T0113374

BARNARD NEW WOMEN POETS SERIES

Edited by Christopher Baswell and Celeste Schenck

1986   *Heredity*
Patricia Storace
With an Introduction by Louise Bernikow

1987   *Laughing at Gravity: Conversations with Isaac Newton*
Elizabeth Socolow
With an Introduction by Marie Ponsot

1988   *The World, the Flesh, and Angels*
Mary B. Campbell
With an Introduction by Carolyn Forché

1989   *Channel*
Barbara Jordan
With an Introduction by Molly Peacock

1990   *All of the Above*
Dorothy Barresi
With an Introduction by Olga Broumas

1991   *The Stenographer's Breakfast*
Frances McCue
With an Introduction by Colleen J. McElroy

1992   *We Are the Young Magicians*
Ruth Forman
With an Introduction by Cherríe Moraga

1993   *That Kind of Danger*
Donna Masini
With an Introduction by Mona Van Duyn

1994   *Straight Out of View*
Joyce Sutphen
With an Introduction by Judith E. Johnson

White Elephants

REETIKA VAZIRANI

White

With an Introduction by Marilyn Hacker

Elephants

Beacon Press
Boston

Beacon Press
25 Beacon Street
Boston, Massachusetts 02108-2892
www.beacon.org

Beacon Press books
are published under the auspices of
the Unitarian Universalist Association of Congregations.

First digital-print edition 2001

Library of Congress Cataloging-in-Publication Data
Vazirani, Reetika
White elephants / Reetika Vazirani ; with an introduction by Marilyn Hacker
p.   cm.—(Barnard new women poets series)
ISBN 0-8070-6833-0
1. Women—United States—Poetry. 2. East Indian Americans—Poetry. 3. India—Poetry. I.
Title. II. Series.
PS3572.A985W48   1996
811´.54—dc20   9545057

For Derek, George, and Jyotika

Contents

Acknowledgments

Grateful acknowledgment is made to the editors of the following publications, in which poems from *White Elephants* first appeared, some in slightly different form:

Agni Review: "Mrs. Biswas Breaks Her Connection with Another Relative"

American Voice: "Amma's Ruby"

Callaloo: "Malik, My First Cousin" 1–5, "Mrs. Biswas," "Mrs. Biswas Gives Advice to a Granddaughter," "Mrs. Biswas Banishes a Female Relative," "Calcutta, for Jai," "Letter to a Husband," "Reading the Poem about the Yew Tree"

International Quarterly: "The Mercator Projection," "The Service"

Journal of the American Medical Association: "Heart Donor"

Kenyon Review: "Mica," "Lobster," "On the Fast Train," "Devi," "Ras Mohun" appeared as "Thinking about Citizenship," "Housekeeping in the New World," "Underground," "In the War"

Literary Review: "White Elephants II"

Nation: "Mrs. Biswas Remembers Mookherjee," "Postcards & Telegrams," "White Oak, 1975," "Into the Capitol," "Chasing Lime"

Parnassus: "Sunday School"

Prairie Schooner: "Mrs. Biswas's Career as a Painter," "The Rajdhani Express," "Star-Reader, Palm-Reader," "White Elephants I," "A Million Balconies"

Salamander: "*Unda-Wala*, the Egg-man," "Dervishes"

Seattle Review: "Mrs. Biswas of Maryland on the Phone"

Sojourner: "The Temple" appeared as "Doctor Vaz"

Excerpts quoted in this book are published in the following:

Carlos Drummond de Andrade, "Looking for Poetry," in *Travelling in the Family: Selected Poems of Carlos Drummond de Andrade*, ed. Thomas Colchie, trans. Mark Strand (New York: Random House). Reprinted by permission of Random House

Li T'ai Po, "Exile's Letter," trans. Ezra Pound, from *Personae*, copyright © 1926 by Ezra Pound. Reprinted by permission of New Directions Publishing Corp.

Antonio Machado, "Songs VI," in *Times Alone: Selected Poems of Antonio Machado*, trans. Robert Bly (Middletown, Conn.: Wesleyan University Press, 1983). Copyright 1983 by Robert Bly. Reprinted by permission of Robert Bly

I would like to thank the Thomas J. Watson Foundation for a grant that enabled me to travel in India in 1984. Thanks also to the Corporation of Yaddo for a residency in 1992 and to the Sewanee Writers' Conference for a scholarship in 1993. Finally, many thanks to my grandparents, Ras Mohun and Sulekha Halder; to Marilyn Hacker; and to my cousins in Bombay.

Introduction

THE LAYERED WEALTH of experience, of exposition, in Reetika Vazirani's first book is almost enough to make a reader overlook the meticulous craft and linguistic compression with which it is written. At a time when the United States becomes daily more synonymous with exclusion, terror of difference, isolation in its own merely-two-hundred-year-old puritanical culture, here is a young writer's book about the intersection of cultures, about the richness and confusion, the conundrums, the music, the flavors, the constant questioning of a genuinely multicultural existence.

Reetika Vazirani writes about "citizenship," in its profoundest sense, that of an engaged humanist acting in the polis, as a state of perpetual becoming. One's name, one's language, one's religion, one's identity are always subject to possible permutation, until one is not sure oneself how to fill out (must one still fill out?) the visa request. Rereading this book, I think of less fortunate "aliens" locked up indefinitely in chartered jails with no rights and no recourse, awaiting deportation to countries that may be as foreign to them as hostile America; of the "Europeanness" of German and Austrian and Polish Jews made hideously moot; of French Jews retroactively deprived of decades-old citizenship under the Occupation and Vichy; of the perversions of "nationalism" at murderous work in Rwanda, in the Balkans, in Vazirani's natal Indian subcontinent. This book's vision is of an antidote to that deadly division and disdain.

Vazirani's work was not unknown to me when I opened her book manuscript among the more than eight hundred submitted to the Barnard competition: the former editor of a literary quarterly is bound to recognize the work of some of the writers who present themselves for such an occasion. But these poems had meant more to me than that. When I first read a group of them, out of the next manila envelope in the unsolicited manuscript pile, I felt that delighted elation of discovery which is the editor's reward. Here was a young poet I'd never heard of before, with a wonderful ear, prosodic confidence, and *stories* to tell which weren't the ones too often repeated in the contents of those manila envelopes. I published her poems. I asked to see more of them. I published more. But I still wasn't prepared for the authority with which this first collection engages and compels the reader with its tales of voyages and languages, its vivid-voiced characters, its unduped absence of nostalgia.

One of the things that most pleases me about this book is that I'm not obliged to write about it in that abstract language often reserved for "poetry." It goes back and calls forward to a different tradition, in which verse is the means, the chosen genre for the presentation of a narrative whose complexity, whose shifts in scene, time, focus, point of view, demand an approach more akin to a verbal equivalent of cinema than to "straightforward" narrative prose. Scenes and, most particularly, characters appear, disappear, reappear in different settings, under a different light; the reader's senses are bombarded with bits of information as in a hologram, until there is a multifaceted, polydimensional whole to consider, lit from within as well as without.

As in any young writer's book, there are antecedents here, notably the poet's mentor Derek Walcott, whose own compression of contradictory worlds (and infallible ear for English inflected through other tongues) is engaged in dialogue in these pages. But there is also something reminiscent of the compassionate humanism of Adrienne Rich, connecting disparate specifics within minute focus, and of the prosody and sensory precision of Elizabeth Bishop, at home everywhere and nowhere in the world, recording her observations of the "foreign" and the "quotidian" with a naturalist's equal bemusement. And it is hard not to recall Robert Lowell's *History* reading the dense and resonant sonnets of Vazirani's "White Elephants" sequence: family history, world history, the artist's coming-of-age and the witness's anguish are shared by both, along with their form.

(It's good to see the sonnet so vivid and vital in the work of emerging writers like Vazirani, Maureen Seaton, Rafael

Campo, Robyn Selman, Jay Rogoff—and to see the place it retains for Tony Harrison, Marilyn Nelson Waniek, Seamus Heaney, among others. For all of them—of us—it's not a "perfect" lyric, but the engine of narrative energy, a frame-by-frame observation of interconnected and mutable contemporary lives.)

The Rajdhani Express is leaving—or is it the Metroliner, or the Concorde? An extraordinary young traveller has extended an invitation to voyage across decades and continents, into an extended family, several cities, a palette of flavors and textures, into the conundrum of language's origin and the constellation of its accomplishments.

Marilyn Hacker

THINKING ABOUT CITIZENSHIP

Don't bring up
your sad and buried childhood.
Don't waver between the mirror
and a fading memory.
What faded was not poetry.
What broke was not crystal.

—Carlos Drummond de Andrade, "Looking for Poetry"

Ras Mohun

in memoriam R. M. H. (1904–1990)

1. THE HALTING FOOT

I hear Bill Hancock's hammer fastening Sheetrock
in our new room, drills gnawing through plywood.
When I meet the workmen early on the steps,
I sense they think my English poor; and one says slowly,
we don't know how to say your name.
A foreign wariness spans our first house, the light
halting foot of one who is being overheard and knows it.
My grandfather, for example, who held three passports,
died with his British clip lapsing into Bengali,
not sure if "condominium" came from Sanskrit or Pali,
and *where is my glossary?* Then *learn much Latinate root,
read property law, buy acreage for passing on.*
Ras Mohun: a plot of grass down Rockville Pike,
pink granite, alien characters drilled in his stone.

2. HAMMERING

Their hammering willful strokes sound like loud
questions: perfect, schooled spondées; but the sound
is work, purpose with purpose, plank to plank.
I hear shipbuilders bending beams at the dock,
Ras Mohun bringing his wife's dowry on deck.
What routes they had taken! From Bombay, the English
sailed Port Outward and Starboard Home (*posh*,
he would tell me), but he'd never mention
Aden up through the Red Sea where the sun
scorched the second-class side. Maybe he didn't
mind, so near Beirut! Or had he hinted
Alexandria, London, then New York?
What brinks of maps, I never questioned him—
yet Mr. Hancock's men hit the nails each time.

3. FOREIGN PRINCES

My passport came at twenty. I renounced
allegiance to another nation and foreign
princes, though my mind's scattered, like one
at customs trying to locate smuggled goods.
Where for instance is *Nani*'s gold?
The workmen stalk down the hall to eat.
Bent on a stack of beams, they're quiet
and leery like those in line for a visa
to the States. If agents one day check my file,
what if it's fake and my I.D. mistaken?
What haunts me still is deportation.
The airport escort and metal detectors,
long line of aliens at passport control,
and warning symbols on revolving doors.

4. THE DOCK

To have survived my life so far and have landed
here, not next door or where tropics cut through cane,
I know, in spite of all I can lie about: languages
I speak, my church affiliation, foreign princes:
that there is nowhere to go and anything is possible.
Emptying a steamer trunk, peeling off ports of call,
rubbing into blurs dates of entry with digits
that were frequently inked and fingerprinted; I recall
newsstand hawkers tapping windshields in traffic—
a throng of new nouns in an immigrant's throat—
coatrack, driveway, detour, street.

Culture shock is not your reflex upon leaving the dock;
it is when you have been a law-abiding citizen
for more than ten years: when someone asks your name
and the name of your religion and your first thought is
I don't know, or you can't remember what you said last time;
you think there is something you forgot to sign:
your oath, for one; and you are positive
that those green-shirted workmen in the room right now
want to take you in for questioning.

5. Ras Mohun's Village

We don't have furniture for the new room.
This lap organ is my grandmother's harmonium
used mainly for singing hymns and Tagore.
This photograph she gave me is the only one marked
"Ras Mohun's village." One workman said it looked
like bluegrass—imagine that—it was of Dacca
sixty years ago. Until America I never knew what it meant
to inherit boulevards between rows of tobacco,
its amber fragrance racing through your own bourbon,
so much furniture you sell some at auction
where the auctioneer's stutter recalls your latest tongue.
I think, well we are compensated by the latitudes—
home is anyplace, first hang your hat,
and I've learned to be limber you must travel light.

6. Above the Garage

Now they're hauling out the extra wood.
The foreman says good-bye, I say good luck.
I will miss them, their heavy boots, logos
on their overalls: *Myrtle Beach, Memphis.*
I like the room painted white, as if they
discovered no fresco up from Pompeii
or Mohenjo-Daro, it doesn't matter: to these
men maybe history's a ruin, which is true.
And every undated photo shines behind glass
in a new room above the garage. Light
is coming through up here. The men took care
not to smudge the panes. As they back out,
I wave wondering how their windy hair
is there for keeps, plying the air like a flag.

PART I: MRS. BISWAS

Parrots recite.
So what?
Can they read the Lord?

—Basavaṇṇa, from "Vacana 125"

Mrs. Biswas

The Taj Mahal brings to mind a fiefdom—it could have been
but a paranoia
among the saddhus got it palmed off, and men in khaki,
like glasses of tea, put all of Darjeeling and two ports
under Rule Britannia's
rule of thumb. "A very practical man, Mountbatten,

"and that's that," Nani Biswas said, resting on her back.
"Khalaas," she had no further
explanation as to why her family lived in seven houses
on the other side of her first world of Bengal.
"To bring you peoples together
I had to take on bleeding ulcer." At Holy Cross

the family gathered what she liked best: purple nasturtiums,
carnations, coleus, orchids.
Her grandchildren admitted she might have been a difficult
woman—you could say they felt henpecked: from her bed,
she kept on giving orders;
she even looked like Indira Gandhi: her colorist left a couple

of gray streaks and rolled the rest into a plate-sized bun.
She was living long,
touch wood: her grandchildren think she will outlive
the whole clan, because she does not hesitate over choices.
Her only lung
gives her no trouble. "Why should it? I am very social type.

"That is that. Touch wood, and do your work." Proud
of an everlasting braid—

thick as a ship's line and dedicated to her mother—she herself
cannot comb it out but has to ring up one after another:
"Comb my hairs and read
that recipe . . . can you pick up twenty air letters?

"You will get a check with some extra, and what is numbers
of Pat and Mrs. Reynold?
They are both two chatterboxes: with my bleeding ulcer
they will send both me and your Nana to the grave;
chatting for one solid
hour each—can you believe? Remember to burn me

"with the phone book. Too much of buk-buk with those
    birdy womens
and far-off relations.
Meantime I will contact my lawyer and sue Arnold Kappler
who I consulted these twenty years. Not only has the doctor
run up my insurance
premiums, but he has ruined my life. Enough, come over,

"my hair is bothering my head." Nani falls asleep
in a reclining chair.
Her grandchild continues to comb or Nani will wake
with memories of other cheatings. She speaks absently
of mustard oil on black hair
and of skin lighteners, mumbles the word "Dark-One" in Bengali,

numbers cousins in Calcutta, Baroda, Jaipur; refers to a sacred
Kerala monument
whose name is almost unpronounceable. She rattles off
a geography of plant life, dinner plans, tautology;
regrets the settlement
on her uncle's house on Park Street, now a crowded mosque.

She scolds a god, possibly Mahakali, the Great One, for tangling
her boot-black hair in a comb.

She says India is India, America is America. In her silver tumbler
run the last rites of her recent dead (for whom she will
have cooked a toothsome lamb):
"Rainu-mashi, Thakur-dada, Philip Biswas Chatterjee . . .

"And then this Tagore made Shantiniketan. Shah Jehan
built the Taj Mahal,
for whom—can you believe?—his wife. We kept our bungalow
on Park Street, you know, Calcutta, very posh area that time.
Then my Nehru did install
your Nana in the embassy, no doubt he deserved it.

"Remember me to everyone. Take your meals on time.
Don't forget to weigh
our air letters before posting abroad. Still you have
to comb my hair. What to do with the silver? Save
it for your wedding day."
When the child has rinsed the favored ivory comb,

Mrs. Biswas is snoring softly: her breath and undone plait
make semicircles of split
pistachios, almonds, and dialect—unthinkable to cut it off
near a photo in which she is prominent
among siblings on the plot
next to Governor Hiren Mukherjee's tennis court.

The child leaves the comb by her Nani's diamonded ear
so that she will have the call
of elephanta, the gurgling stream of her perpetual hair.
Mrs. Biswas promised, when her mother died, her braid would
    grow longer
than the spine of a practical
man, longer than the reign of an ordinary queen.

Mrs. Biswas Banishes a Female Relative

That is not the way.
That is not the way to behave.
What kind of way is that to behave.
Now she has no shame.
We don't know her anymore.
How can we know her this way.

Once she knew what was shame.
She was the steady one.
How unsteady she has become.
She is not my granddaughter.
Let her wander, then.
Let her clothes grow thin.

Mrs. Biswas Gives Advice
to a Granddaughter

What did I learn in Loretto College?
Plenty. Bible and economy,
Botany, arts, and culture.
Book knowledge was advisable.
(Do not throw yourself under
The wheels of *Jaganatha*—
The English call it Juggernaut,
But what is that to me?)

Learn to live where you are
And forget about the local myths,
They will only fool you.
When you are older, you too
Can lecture to your children;
Meanwhile finish your reading,
And be quick with your degree—
What can you do with it? Teach reading?

Thus, I suggest you attend
The parties. And keep a tidy place:
Guests will show up for colddrinks
And tea. Offer savoury snacks
With something sweet: shondesh
Or bakery cakes. In Calcutta
We craved the English cakes
(Now-days any type will do).

But mainly, serve your food on time,
And speak on the current topics.
Your Nana has lived for eighty years,

You could have taken his words
Of knowledge, but now he is
Watching the news. It is late—
Let me get his pajamas;
You sit here I am coming.

Mrs. Biswas Goes through
a Photo Album

1. HOLIDAYS AT LAKE NAGEEN, 1925–1938

You see us in this picture,
four girls with matching frocks,
four cousin-brothers wearing cricket caps
all at Kashmir on holiday.
We hired a boat with thirteen
rooms and took our own cook, Tirupati.

2. CHRISTIAN LIFE

It was fresh air days, and streets
were clear for evening walks,
not like problems we are having now,
Hindus rioting with Musselman.
We were Baptists from the start
though we respected goddess Kali,
very prominent goddess in Calcutta
seen in every temple.
We snapped her photo at *Durga Puja*.
Whatever you may think of it,
we retained our Christianity.
And when we walked outdoors at eight
in the evening, Mashi wore her crucifix
outside her sari blouse, and we walked
with the Buntings who had lately
turned to be Jesuits.

3. BUSINESS LIFE

You ask about the childhood days—
you recall my father died.
His brother had a soda factory

so we lived with Uncle Jiten,
such a house he kept on Park Street.
(See nine cousins on the marble stairs.)
And he dispensed our pocket money
at the season's final cricket match;
we stood behind the soda sellers
and gathered the bottlecaps:
one anna per dozen, and the coins
among us lasted all year.

4. MARRIAGE

My sister keeps the college photos
so this next one is my marriage day:
note the length of receiving line,
so large was our family
even I cannot recall the names.
Some say numerous impostors joined
to partake of our prestige.
The Governor himself arranged
the date; he even matched your Nana
to me—such marvelous governors
we had those times. My portrait
was shown at the Reception Hall.
Photos are one thing, but painted
canvas—only that one kept my beauty.

Mrs. Biswas's Career as a Painter

After school, Mr. Chandana gave us lessons
on painting and the fall of light on copper vessels.
To show what shadows were, he swayed his wrist and
hand, or twisted
them like a swimming minnow under the pots' array.

(And I was known for whispering, why not
he take up oceanography?) But I was caught
and made to sit in front near Chandana,
and under the
sketch of pots I mixed an oval of dark paints.

I finished two *barthans* that season, and he said
I hadn't seen how the shadows, in delicate tones, spread
only slightly underneath. One vessel's bulge
was not so huge
on the tablecloth at the three o'clock hour

when the sun is fairly overhead. But what did he
know? The cloth was stained when Mrs. Bannerjee
came to lunch (our next-door neighbor's aunt
with some complaint
about the hubbub from our house—nine children in and
    out all day).

Like Chandana, she pushed her hand and tipped
a cup of tea onto the lace crochet and spoiled it—
Belgian lace from the Consul General. Mashi
said it didn't matter;
but who can overlook the indignity of insult, then stain,

as when the sun had burned my feet between
the sandal straps, and showed that my being out at noon
was the act of an ill-bred wastrel type, a foolish
inauspicious
schoolgirl; and that my bad luck would mar my reputation.

So I informed Chandana that if the shade I drew
was too great for the vessel in the afternoon,
it was only to hide that unmannerly
woman's pool of tea
and nothing more. But on the basis of that mistake,

my painting was held up as the false way
of making light suit the student's lazy eye;
and I was taken out of the Artists' Guild,
being so unskilled
and even rude to our instructor, and was later trans-

ferred to flower arrangement as a charity volunteer.

Mrs. Biswas Remembers Mookherjee

Of course I remember Mookherjee—
his father was my father's friend.
And when Mookherjee was twenty-one,
he visited me after school.
Of course I remember.
He wanted a wife.
He was through with university
and planned to enter business sending
tea to States, or tea to France.

But then he disappeared,
and his parents made excuses—
he went to London to study law;
he's learning shipping in Hong Kong. . . .
All lies, all lies, I knew.
He went to Christian Seminary;
and when I saw him again, he bowed
his head and said he must attend
to a baptism, but how was I?
Oh I was very well, I said.

But I knew at once what his tone
was—not out of respect for God;
but because those days he came to me,
fourteen times I refused his hand.
And for this Mookherjee is sitting
all his life in the cloak intent
on his devotions and the other world.

Mrs. Biswas Breaks Her Connection
with Another Relative

Nobody can please her except God,
she is that type of girl.

This is what news I have heard:
she is expecting only seven months
after the wedding.
Did she come to my house
to tell me of the wedding?
No, she phoned me up.
She is a daring girl—
from the beginning when she came
to this country she was always
rebellious and disobedient.
Who can instruct her
who has her own ideas on life? For that,
I am breaking my connection.
Nobody can please her except God,
she is that type of girl.

Mrs. Biswas of Maryland on the Phone

I.

That Sindhi boy is keen on you.
I saw his mother at Sari Town;
nowadays she is chubby as fruit,
worrying constantly for her son.
I discussed that you are up at school
just like your Nana was. Now he is lame,
and any second he could fall,
he rambles about lorries on our road,
hiccups for several days at a time,
only three Bengali words he says to me.
I am with your Nana this century
so I know what it is to be married.

II.

Are your foods good in Cambridge?
You are getting mustard seed and cabbage?
If not, I can send you mustard seed
by post, but for delays on this end;
I am thinking worldwide postal strike—
last month critical letter to X
of D.C. bank, regarding Nana's checks,
came back to me with Philippine postmark.
Mix-ups like India only but very
much worse: last week I sent my sari
to new dry cleaner, and I was in shock
to be billed for two tablecloths.

III.

I must buy eighteen nylon saris
and Walkmans for my India trip;

hope customs won't take my batteries.
For years I collected lipsticks to give—
Avon, Ultima, and Maybelline;
I ordered heart attack tablets
and Dramamine pills—handy for seven-day
weddings of Hindus; and I retain fluid;
lately my thumb expanded to such an extent,
I answer the phone with my oven mit.
Labana, Cheekoo, paying respects: believe me,
they're hinting of fashions from Delhi.

IV.

You do one thing: come with me to Delhi
while Blue Cross is carrying my health;
I must procure your husband or else
you settle on that Sindhi boy, no doubt
his father is leading in pathology
(and their import business is nationwide).
At twenty-one I finished botany
and engaged. You are nearly twenty-eight,
reading, reading, how do you live,
you will get cataracts from scholarship;
no money, then you go blind. Your Nana was
a scholar, but that Sindhi, tsch, clever in accounts.

PART II: THE RAJDHANI EXPRESS

in memory of A. K. Ramanujan (1929–1993)

Tō So-kiu of Rakuyō, ancient friend, Chancellor Gen.
Now I remember that you built me a special tavern
By the south side of the bridge at Ten-shin.

—Li T'ai Po, "Exile's Letter"

Reading the Poem about the Yew Tree

Reading the poem about the yew tree,
I realize I do not recall the trees of my youth,
the particular leafy shapes and blooming seasons and their
    moist odors in the heat.
I could look them up in a tree guide
and mend the holes in my memory—
but then it would not be my memory,
it would be the guide's.

All I remember today is the rapid chatter
of tea-colored women,
their plump arms, fingers reaching out
to pinch us when we were small;
lips passing hushed remarks
about others in the town, like branches shifting in the wind.
The grown-ups talked as if they hadn't heard
any local news but had to inquire after rumors.
You mean to say she is tolerating that scoundrel Gopal?
(though they'd all been to the wedding).
And their voices always verged on anticipation,
as if waiting for a great event to unfold—
a heavy rain to cool the grass
or the breeze with some news.
But they were indoors perpetually expecting another guest
    to arrive,
so that when the somebody appeared
they would congratulate the guest in unison:
See that, we were just speaking of you,
you will live long.

Now, planning a trip to my homeplace,
I'm told our friends are gone, have moved or passed away.
But I imagine the same kinds of trees are growing now as then,
and they will be expecting me when I arrive.

To Tara

I am writing to you, Tara,
because now that you have left White Oak
it occurs to me that your journey at twenty-one,
thousands of miles east,
seems like mine thirty years ago
when I went the other way; from school in Mussoorie,
north of Delhi, to Women's College in North Carolina.
No one we knew had been there; I had only a brochure
which showed red buildings, white columns, blue sky—
it looked new. Not like Red Fort
where the air is yellow like a paper one day in the sun.
I took the train to Bombay and in those days
we sailed to Lebanon, then flew to Paris.
Probably I have not told you about that trip,
not enough, and now it is late to answer questions
you asked repeatedly, for a dozen years.
You may wonder what right has an absent mother to
    approach you now.
Your cousin told me you were staying in Delhi
with Uncle Marwah, so I am sending this letter to him.
        He received me before you were born,
        and we exchanged garlands as we would today.

                    *   *   *

Of my trip, I remember in Paris someone forgot to save
for the final fee and was sent back.
Here are enough dollars to change into rupees—
there'll be an airport tax—
            change the money at a bank.
And don't photograph the crafts or strangers—
don't sit with anyone's luggage.

As I write to you, it is not hard to remember my departure—
the corridors were swamped;
luggage and bottled drinks, magazines, cigarettes—they
    free you!
Dollies were sharp and rusty but it didn't matter,
there were porters at every step,
and even after sixteen years in India,
I was always astonished to see a thin man
hoist a steel trunk on his back and smoke a *bidi*
at the same time—
        how did he breathe?

And right before me, a soldier spoke to a stranger
who had briskly read a copy of the afternoon paper:
they talked about the British leaving—
about the fairly recent civil war—(we were in '55,
Partition was '47, as if that is everything!).
So I imagine where you are,
somebody is distraught about the Golden Temple crisis:
that the army found jewelry, muskets, gin, and harlots
in the sacred chambers; Sikh militants
who have even printed their own currency,
issued passports in their new name of Khalistan.
I regret you cannot visit Punjab.
The embassy says the border is sealed.
In Patiala, our phone number was eight-eight-eight;
everyone knew us, there wasn't anyone we didn't know.

And yet there is Bangladesh, India, Pakistan:
no nation but more names for it,
and what remains of the jewel in the crown—
holes where the Taj held diamonds—
are karats of Sanskrit and Dravidian names—
Punjab, Gujarat, Bengal, Kerala—from the train
        you can see everything—
but the inner provinces split as under a jeweler's cut;
so let Khalistan take its place in the history of gems.

*   *   *

It is not easy to travel—
but what can replace it, that is what I ask myself,
because everything was not marriage, though we wished for it.
        I was sixteen, a girl, accompanied for four weeks,
            my trip was nothing like yours, a few Mondays,
but if I had never ventured that once across the world,
even my dreams would lack.
I had hoped this trip for you:
hoped it would be shorter, taken in better times.
So if you are in Delhi during riots,
go north to the mountains,
to Woodstock School in Mussoorie—
        Mrs. Bhatia will meet you—
            she wrote me that you nearly came once before;
get past Punjab
or whatever they call it years from now.
North of there we schoolchildren camped.
There must still be zinc roofs to sit under in the rain
and shards of mica littering the ground.

        *   *   *

I often look at the atlas.
Maps have more lines in them now.
How could the English have known they were smarter
than they were?—learning tactics from an epic let's say.

Maybe if I read the Mahabharata scene by scene
I wouldn't be impressed anymore by the plot:
a game of dice, heros at odds with fate,
the insulted warriors. . . .
When we were very young we based our lives on these episodes.
We thought of duty and action in terms of *Kurukshetra*,
the field of battle, and of the *Gita*—
a spangled chariot taking a question to the moon—
        what we would achieve—.

I am old and it is quick.
I'm thinking *You*: less than half my age. How can that be?

A year and two oceans between us.
What is waiting at your next stop?
The kohl-dark tarmac,
distances slimmed by flight, its smoky arc above the world;
the unrelenting wheel—.

Or could it be windows of mica on handloom cloth?
Heat glistening on the runway that day I waited for clearance?

Or what with travel the heart becomes,
not your emerald birthstone—
the gems won't last till then—
but a pomegranate, hard to get at and ripe.

       Until the next, I wish you well, Tara.
       In a few weeks your sister is graduating
       and Ashok is moving to Delaware.

Letter to a Husband

Fifth day past the full moon you ended
fourteen years with Rama in the forest.
I took the children to another house.
It seemed useless to wait for a shadow
that falls on the road at five but doesn't come in.

You wore your oldest sandals. Are they broken now?
One night the ones you left I put out at the temple.
Various men must be wearing them—
I don't even know who they are.
As for the city,
the courtesans prepare annually for your arrival.
They do not think of my position.
Like you, they never felt the taut skin
of this native land burdened by so much waiting;
and all along, your brother kept a seat for you at
          Nandigram,
white umbrella of the state. Therefore our eldest, Govindas,
will not assume your tasks until council reconvenes.

I am teaching at the school near Palika Bazaar,
so crowded it has become,
but I have seen all five children through,
and with their classmates also gone,
it is less well known I am your wife.
Lately the students confuse me with Memsahib Arvinda;
she has taken up teaching, too old to entertain—
you remember her?—
favored by all your brothers who kept her house
on the western compound near the *mali*'s house.
I knew everything but didn't say.

Sometimes I see her across the *maidan* in her white sari.
One day I will approach her. I have lost only you.
How many must be gone from her!

 So I give this letter to the son of your harness-keeper
 who still speaks as if you are coming through the gate.
 And when you receive this,
 go to her: at dusk, she waits in the clearing
 where the same *mali* plants too many marigolds
 because the champak trees never took root.

The Rajdhani Express

I. KHAR TO CHURCHGATE

Protests painted on walls by the railway.
A child sleeps in a red motor-cum-parcel van.
Inside a printed sign:

Unescorted young students
depend upon you for protection.
Please look after them.

II. VICTORIA TERMINUS

Behind the bus stands hoot all the trains:
a porter bustles through crowds with a trunk
on his head, as the newlyweds dodge after him;
and people pour out of V. T.
like monsoon rain from the mouth of a gargoyle.

III. NARAIN DHABOLKER ROAD

Uniformed children with cricket bats shout,
slap the walls, waiting for the lift
in Government Officers Flat on Malabar Hill.
They play hooky from school
and run toward the hawkers:
their envelopes, ink pens, and roasted nuts
in newspaper cones—
and the clatter of money in cans!

IV. COOPERAGE ROAD

Balconies peer toward three black women
with oiled buns. Men stalk by others
on motorbikes, some men looking for work.

A lentil hawker glares at his customer,
sells her a kilo of ordinary pulse.
At dusk, he will sneak home on a local train.

V. Near Baroda

The bearer asks the young Australian,
"Sahib, you are taking tea?"
He asks for a Coca-Cola with ice.
The bearer brings a bottled Thumbs-Up.
The traveller smells it for something alien.
At dark, the boy sleeps on his side, nobody's kin—
and it's seven hours to the next tea call.
The train cuts through villages of grain.

VI. Lotana Station

Coconut palms shoot branchlessly up
with tiny tufted tops; some bend sideways, strain,
frozen where the wind went.
The citrus sun flashes on window panes,
and a few early risers see
a coconut palm growing out of a hardwood tree.

VII. Vadodara Station

I have lived here before.
Kulfi melts across the sky.
Plains, longer than a sari's hem,
stretch northward, cropless and rich.

Letter to a Cousin

for Varsha

Bhabhi said this yogurt came from Amma's yogurt:
she brought it herself, one spoonful in a silver box
when they came from Karachi, before Sindhis dispersed
into the trade centers: Hong Kong, Bombay, London,
New York; before the five-fingered Indus
sprung up geyserlike and the splashes peopled
other cities and ports.

We shelled peas and talked about family things,
your feet up on my chair, and the pods themselves
like this jumbled genealogy:
Hong Kong, Bombay, London, New York. . . .
Our fathers were brothers, and somehow
there is a trace of Amma's yogurt in all of this,
house of Jethanand Tarachand.

You trailed off the balcony
shaking a towel near a wet, white sari
murmuring what I never thought you knew,
measured and slow like a school book rhyme
with the last line lost: Sunder Jethanand,
Jethanand Tarachand, Tarachand Hiranand,
Hiranand Thirtadas—

I waited for you to finish:—you said,
Baba's sister remembers the rest—:
but at least the outline is there: our fathers
were brothers; and their mother, Amma,
I imagine she preserved things, like this box of yogurt
in a linen napkin, since it was her mother's yogurt,
white as pressed silk saris that time.

We talked on of bronze saucers and plates
sold in Ulasnagar for a pittance,
at a time when school books and new shoes
meant much more than this backward looking
at heirlooms, or investments
we could have had today—gold,
and the old currency melted into spoons.

I snapped the last pod. You poured green water
over the rail, like a Holi scare, and reminded me
that the old ones say we younger ones
would rather forget Kalyan; and in two generations,
maybe one, the children will not know Sindhi,
or red-rice *puri* and fried *brinjohl*,
or why we have such Sindhi names.

Calcutta, for Jai

At first my hostess sent me on my own
for flowers, cabbages, and spice,
which I smelt among fragrant loads upon

crates, handled by girls wearing glass
bracelets and bright skirts at the tented
market near Ballygunge—so that it was

odd after a week to have you as a mentor
of sorts; to tour your news headquarters
and think news when I was bent on

kilos of *phul* and *phul-gobi*, bottles of *acchar*.
And you, preoccupied with Rainu
on your staff, the youngest reporter,

who said she might agree to marry you,
left you no confidence because she had
a wide choice (her father had to interview

five men that month). She tried to hide
her suspicion of me, and I assured her I
was Mrs. Chowdhury's guest and you were my guide.

And she knew Mrs. Chowdhury extremely
well, Mrs. P. K. Chowdhury, the very one!
(though I can't remember how). Did I tell you we

met in the hall before she took the train
to Serampore on assignment? She is lovelier
than what they say of Bengali women,

and quite smart. So I understood her cavalier
attitude:—she was poised on a moment of terrific
bounty—to marry someone famous in Calcutta!

And then we weaved through the extraordinary traffic,
you and I, went across town past the Brit-
ish monuments to your old school's cricket

field, where a white ball rolled from wrist
to bat, and the bowler suddenly shouted
huzza-huzza-huzza-Ram! a hit

so unexpected the applause resounded
as in a stadium into the seated crowd,
and every black bird was flying keenly out and

over Karaya Road. Then, as a wedding parade
clamored on another street, we said good-bye.

Next day, when the electricity cut off as it did,

you said, each noon on that block of high
windows, we leaned again on the warm railing
of a balcony where we talked easily

of everything but the sprawling
city you have been living in for more than
thirty years you said; as if that were too long—

(and I knew you felt she might see us then
freely talking, but she didn't, she was
out of town). And that week in your car and on

foot in Calcutta, it became my favorite place
in India: the noisy roads I love
in it are splendid and dangerous,

and I have learned that to live
there you have to know who you are.
Thank you for showing me the city life—.

And when you have a moment, write me your
news. Don't forget to tell me what Rainu decides;
and if she says no, don't blame her,

she's young; don't blame yourself for having tried,
and don't think she saw us. Mrs. Chowdhury says,
in Calcutta the chance of being recognized

is so slight, even an out-of-doors tryst has,
to conceal it, the noises
of theaters, markets, and alleyways.

Jai, who knows who knocked or who was next
door with whom talking all night in low voices,
who slept alone and who couldn't rest.

Star-Reader, Palm-Reader

At Central Library in Bombay, my eldest cousin
Shyam was sifting through a stack of post-
colonial books on manufacturing, the best
technique for polishing plastic beads
(ongoing research for the Geeta Gem Factory).
But he was dying to read the astrology guides;
and, fixing his eyes on a chart, some dim star,
he began speaking to me of a family curse.
Every eldest daughter's eldest daughter
suffered from it: Nani Kadam, Savatri,
now Harmeen: not one could retain her husband.
There was polio, suicide, now divorce.

But I was the *second* daughter of an eldest one,
I was not pursuing marriage. "Don't mind it,"
he said. "Give the day and minute you were born.
Quick, the birth certificate."
                                    It was abroad.
So he hit my hand and said, "Show me——."

"Good," he said, "you'll be celibate, disease
will be fairly minor and you'll be rich
for several years. This is not bad fate."
Then he put away the books and led me through
the city's glittering streets to celebrate.

PART III: WHITE ELEPHANTS

in memory of my father
S. J. V. (1929–1974)

Night of Castille;
the poem is spoken,
or, better, not spoken.
When everyone is sleeping,
I'll go to the window.

—Antonio Machado, "Songs VI"

You stand, Malik, my first cousin, beyond
drink, without a thought for the night, or how
the moon shines on the crescent of a face,
between the balcony and blasting bath water,
half an angry lime, no tonic, and no towel.
Gin's gone to waste with your Muslim friends
on New Year's. Baba's fourteen years dead.
It shows a grandson's naked lack of respect:
drinks in his house: it isn't our New Year.
Alcohol can be so loud. Now, nothing.
No one else is in the flat. You look at me
like the last chance a Mirchandani's got
either to beget the next generation of traders;
or, like the conqueror, to emigrate.

[2]

Your wife has gone to Baroda on holiday.
In spite of the eagle on my new passport,
you don't call me American. I speak Hindi
better than your Bombay *paan-wala* patois
which, like Chowpatty Beach, is riotous
as customs is everywhere. I can't stay
in India longer: my visa ran out and I know
you are trying to decide whether to bathe
or have me take you West. Or, is it just
that you want to leave your Hyderabadi wife?
And you will get a Green Card, a condo
in New Jersey, set up an export firm,
keep me in Piscataway; when the coast
is clear, go to India and come back.

[3]

I watched you pray before the blue head of Ganesh.
I heard our great-aunt say *Bhagwan kai saath.*
Go with God. How many times has she said to you
Go with God?—as if you were not going with God,
but with someone else, bewildered, abroad. . . .
When you make another life on the other side
of earth, will you tell a soul that you, a Sindhi,
have two wives like your two tongues—
and know that all our virginity is undone
as you teach me your hodge-podge language,
mix Muslim privileges with our Hindu ways;
keep two wives: not Lakshmi, but Lakshmi and me?
You crossbreed gods like strains of wheat and rice,
mix Allah with Brahma and Vishnu and Mahesh.

[4]

You remember driving on Shirdi Road
behind a tumbling green village lorry
and barebacked men tossing overripe fruit—
lychee peels and tusklike white radishes—
as if Ganesh would rise from that compost;
Parvathi conceiving him all alone.
We parked under a tamarind tree, your hot
cream-colored Padmini Fiat on the way back
from the ashram of that thin village prophet
whom our grandfather had prodigious belief in.
There was nothing suspicious about it;
discretion these days is so damn easy,
but even then it was too late to say,
Malik, Malik, Malik, you're my cousin.

[5]

To tell you honestly, it can't happen,
can it? It's just a thought that you'd turn
your life upside-down. I look at you between
the balcony and blasting bath water,
land and the Arabian Sea, your marketplace
jargon and our Karachi Sindhi speech.
You come forward sucking half an angry lime.
I say, sailor, we are both marooned on this beach.
Maybe we will make love, Malik, next October,
or better yet, let's keep it open: another time—
when we are more distant cousins and your charm
will have traversed the citrus path of a bee in warm
Karnataka or California. God speed and God bless
the empty spaces, calendars, maps, your expectant face.

Sunder Jethanand: Jeth is your father;
Sunder is a remnant of Alexander
whose legions forged through Peshawar hills
and left their names. A rose bloomed
in Konya. That limber Sufi, Jalaluddin,
wrote, "Read the story of the ascension
from the cheek of the beloved." And you
didn't believe a couplet could help you;
nor Rumi's waterwheeling dervishes—
a wool shawl spinning until it knows it is
becoming Alexander, Sekander, Sunder
in a thousand years. How much sooner
water erodes rock or details fade.
Your name stays like a feature of my mind.

I began thus: a Rajdhani Express:
Delhi, Howrah, Victoria Terminus—
in India I coursed a triangular route
from cousin to cousin despite the fall heat
and slow mail; the clutter of my dowry
dwindled, which freed me to write, not about me,
or you, or a vegetarian Thursday,
but about how to leave and where to stay.
The older ones said I was you. I pored
over maps and train tables, powdered the floor
for *rangoli*, strung lights in December;
Divali, lipstick, girls in *ghagras* under
a bridge. Imagine a daughter of yours
bewildered among aunts and blurry station doors.

Many cringed because Amma gave gems
to relations according to her whim.
At her sons' weddings she brought each bride
diamonds, reticence, filigree in gold;
and the weddings were long, and women wore tiers
of hand-strung pearls and some wore sapphires,
as if Seeta's trail of gems was seen again—
clues dropped from a fleeing chariot
so that her husband, the prince, would follow them.

Amma passed a ruby through my mother to me.
It fits my ring finger, and suitors think I'm engaged.
And it's odd because this stone was found
flawed at the markets by Amma's maid
who couldn't trade it for a decent fish.

I rode through Bombay, my *kemize* pressed in
a bus, all of us up to the window's hinge.
Billboard of lovers: Naseerudin and Nargis
from the films. In doorways, teenage girls
like sultanas read magazines of movie stars.
Even loitering, there were roles to play.
Heroine. *Goonda.* An old rowhouse whore's
loving laughter skittered around her skirt
in the red-light district by the bridge.
Chiffon *chuunis* swished over balconies
like a breeze lifting off the coast,
while every *wala* whistled hit songs
at girls approaching customers with ease.
Bright nights known to the harsh horns of taxis.

A Father's Portrait
Chowpatty Beach, Bombay

Your brothers still use Hindi slang when they
bargain with hawkers for *kulfi, chat,*
and *bhel,* but they tell me you always got
the lowest price in that jargon. Just twenty,
you slipped into the diction of doctors,
priests, and taxi drivers. Your fluency
was like the tide, I'm told, a gift which took
its source from the moon with its million names:
poonam, som, chandrama. . . . Your brothers
loved your talent with languages; they wished
you luck. But what about you—new in
Chicago and back in school? You wrote
at a snail's pace, stuttered American
English and tried to hide the foreign nouns.

[11]

But here in your brother's flat in Colaba
it doesn't matter—it's as if you never
left but somewhat quieter. And now
fifteen years later we're going
to Chowpatty Beach again tomorrow,
when the sun goes down
past India Gate at Apollo
Bunder, and Dada will mention when you
were in town, and how you saved some pocket
change, and swapped the easy riot
of your gags with hawkers who finally
gave in, because you were lively
and of their mettle, and they'd cut
their profits to have you come around.

Her father is your father: my aunt,
your eldest sister, Devi, meaning light.
Eight twenty-two-karat bangles rang
on her wrist as she inched between her bed,
the basin, a drawstring pouch of village gold.
Incense smeared from her feet on the floor
spreading prayers like spores, bangles chinking to and fro.

When I arrived in Bombay, she was waiting
for me on a cot sitting like a cup of milk.
And I remember this: that she was serene,
speaking only one language, oiling her hair
for holidays and prayers, pressing her silk
on me, my comfort; keeping the temple flame
lit amid garlands, and living up to her name.

[13]   The Temple
                                   Maryland, 1974

One thing everyone knew you could do was talk.
"Doctor? Heavy accent? O that's Vaz."
You were Aquarian, water-bearer.
What got hold of you? Probably air; lack
of air, and gripping a temple's incensed other-
worldly turf, Satya Sai Baba Nivas,
a shrine you assembled in your son's walk-
in closet, a room with wall-to-wall carpet;
red, white, and blue curtains and flags. But
inside the temple was hammered brass, a candle,
silver, glass, and filigree bookmarks
clipping Sindhi script with an ivory tusk.
Everything shone, touched by sandal,
agarbati, rose water, and your own musk.

New to us: White Elephant Sale ads
and friends who'd never seen an elephant
except at the zoo, never seen one dance
at the market or loiter in a field.
They didn't know that if a boy tells a girl
she walks like an elephant, it means she
lured him with her sophisticated gait.
Now, when asked about India, I show
the garlanded creatures on the record stand,
an array of sandalwood carved by hand
in Mysore, a whole tusk in a chip of ivory,
the mother with her thick trunk raised
and the calves running after as if they
lead a pilgrimage or a parade.

[15]   Thanksgiving at the Cranberry Bog

Collecting firewood on a breezy trail
you nod to me intently and with good will,
venerable neighbor, shade of my father
in the year of feasts three thousand and ten.
Of course in this fog, your hair is grayer,
and your features have lost their distinction,
though the day still seems a surprise: the parade
before Thanksgiving dinner, the red
flood of the bog pulling in its saris
to greet us: not in Sind but in a country
unnaturally fruitful as years are long;
and many share news of migrations and bring
food for the meal, and cousins who've crossed two
continents speak as if we'd never left them long ago.

[16]　　　　　*Unda-wala*, the Eggman
　　　　　　　　　Patiala, Punjab

They say I waited at the windowsill
for Peace Corps man to cycle up with eggs;
that he was fond of me and I loved him.
How can that be?—*unda-wala* and me
(I was just four). But where did his eggs go,
and did he live with the Maharaja,
or did he live with others in a house like ours?
I don't know; I only looked for him.

My parents thought him charming and well read;
perhaps he was from an academy.
He told them to take us to America
where there is a better chance.
Now we are here. O you *unda-wala*,
still cycling around in Patiala!

[17]　　　Housekeeping in the New World
　　　　　　　　　Maryland, 1969

She cut her hair and joined a writing class.
But odder still to him, she never wrote
to relatives. She bought foreign plants
and rooted vines on every windowsill,
used Latin names for flowers, wore slacks
not saris, and turned on a Joplin rag
or Sousa drill, and frequently the vacuum,
sucking footsteps out (as if for one
moment the children would disappear)—

　　　　　　　　　　　　and him:
he craved *baingan* fried and *kofta* curry.
He didn't count her sloppy joes as food,
the canned sauce and bread from plastic wrap—
or frozen *subzi* boiled until the taste
returned to the nothing smell of steam.

In the kitchen hung the Mercator map.
My father said it showed a proper bulge,
and some regions didn't look too little—
Sind or Punjab; and maybe Flanders too,
home of Mr. Mercator. I knew where Flanders
used to be, the gold brocade area
in my history book. *Hello there Mister*
Map Inventor! (though we were not to wave
during meals). But when my father glanced
at the map, I'd turn and look at it too:
the lands looked pale on our wall; but the lines,
fine as hair, were airborne somehow—concave
or convex, they had the run of the place,
and the longitudes coincided at the poles.

He and I sat across the round table
like east and west. Our eyes moved parallel
to the table's rim, as dotted lines
in midair, Tropic of Capricorn, or
the tropic of our lives as far as lives go—
so that when I would grow and sit very tall,
my eye level to his eye level,
wouldn't we too coincide? Not randomly,
but like a pin pushed into a city
we knew well. It was latitude
we wanted from our map—we wanted
to skim the Projection's hairline arcs
on a plane with a long anchor gliding
over continents, then taking hold.

Dinner rules went like this: Don't squirm.
Sit straight. Say please. Chew
twenty times, but don't tap your feet.
Never ask for candy; it rots the mouth—
think of the rumors we'd start around here:
the dentist's children lost their teeth.
(And without teeth, we'd never talk; we'd howl
like wolves, you warned.) The lack of sugar
meant thrift to you. You wanted patients who
could pay, not your straggly brood with holes
for molars waiting at your clinic door.
You explained the punishments; so we chewed
a lot, sat poker-straight until excused.
At night we hid our candy in our shoes.

[21]   The Smell of Leather

He'd round up five of us and any child
who happened to be over. We piled
into the wagon and crossed town to Quincy's
Outlet, a barn building with colored lights;
and the tall, gaunt shoeman would press our toes
one by one, our feet in his big slide-rule-
like shoe sizer. We were flushed by the spree,
and we'd drive home smelling like leather.

But our friends' parents would always bring
the boxes kindly back—*we wish you hadn't;*
as it is, Little X has too many shoes.
It bothered him to stand there: neighbors empty-handed
in his hall, his own intentions half misunderstood—
shoes lacked as a boy, recalled as a father.

53

Mummy said *mali* dug the shelter
fourteen feet by ten by ten. For three
days his head went lower down until
I only saw a batch of dirt, roots
and stone by the edge of the hole.
Next, like a needle, the ladder slipped in,
and we all went out to see our box of air
in the earth; too far to hop down.
I saw wicker seats, small like baskets,
waiting for us on the damp floor. At night,
when the sirens finally blared, we couldn't
hear the goats complain about the fence.
Goats, goats! they wanted to tag along
with us, but we left them bleating on the lawn.

[23]

And my gray, shaggy terrier, Lady, where
did she sit? With me no doubt on the stool
from home, to be still on underground.
To please her I thought the moon could be
our pocket money; we'd pay a black taxi
to drop us at the English shops or Connaught
Circus for *dupatta* and golden shoes—
for all we wished, we'd take along rupees.
But she would badger me and fidget
to reach the ladder up to the yellow moon.
Mummy said, "Ssshhh, don't be anxious,
we'll go back up when the sirens stop,
and you must discipline your dog and don't
talk so much, it's now past ten o'clock."

[24]

Awake in two rows there's Daddy, Mum,
and Deepi; then *chota-bhai*, Lady, and me.
We don't talk because of the dark hour
in the earth. Nothing to tell Lady now,
no taxi ride and no flying off with
the pilot circling over our bungalow.
I stroke Lady quietly while flashlights
light our shirts a queer organza white
at that depth, Himalayan snow I'd glimpsed
in books: I remembered Sir Edmund
with a striped pennant, and his woolly dogs
rushing up the mountain breathing fog
onto the moon. Then Lady and I, we were
dazzled to be up at night deep in the ground.

[25]   In the War
                                  Patiala, Punjab, 1966–67

I later learned we ate our milking goats
when meat was scarce in the war,
and that our houseboy, Harichand,
had to slaughter them and that he was not
to stay in the shelter during air raids—
he had lice, a loud voice, bad manners,
and the stupidity to linger in the sun.

Sometimes, in the garage, he'd be beaten
for riding Daddy's scooter through town,
spending stolen coins on gin, or dozing
on the lawn. In '66, Hari quit without
a word. We left to inquire at his village.
The Army was moving through, choosing boys,
and Hari rode a green bus to the western border.

Most week-ends, surgeons came for lamb and raita,
masala, rice, and *pista-badam* custard.
American jokes in your Indian accent
brought the whole room hiccups. Laughter was
your chance to check teeth; wisecracks were,
who would have known, a sign of distress—
jokes in a new idiom meant the loss
of another tongue. Your face looked spent
on pure work, a seven-headed panic—
patients waiting, a clinic full of glass.
Doctor, your good nature and dentistry
shattered laughs like mica and lab formica:
a horde of mirrored smiles became more densely
packed over a quarter-acre yard.

I don't think you ever got used to crabs
whose claws you extracted with dental forceps.
You preferred cut-up meat with *fulkas*,
but your Karachi youth could not resist
the sea. The Chesapeake's Cream of Wheat
sand was ample enough to burrow in,
so you went yearly to be buried and burned,
to crawl out of it scorched and peeled
like a spiced shrimp, a pallmall mallet
sent from Somerset or a lobster against
the timer, stubborn, done-for, refusing steam.
Resident Alien, it was your own dream
to leave the refugee camp with your bride.
An immigrant is a kind of suicide.

The blue-haired ladies thought us refugees:
Asian pagans disheveled in the pew,
blatant and tardy; then the blue-eyed gaze.
You bellowed en route that the sermon would start,
photographed the church in a new country,
steeple recently hoisted, a turn-of-the-century house.
Two thousand years of Jesus Christ. We blew it,
Father, White Oak was an accident:
gods and Gods and Kodak Ektachrome;
Vishnu, Zeus, and Moses bore a trident,
a tablet, a Hindu text, a Christian hymn.
We ad-lib it all. What's left is a retina:
the worship of snapshots crammed in an album,
a bicentennial flush with millennia.

We might've been better off somewhere else,
passing through in caravan, on elephant.
Here, white elephants seemed odd to us.
As if elephants they also show up as white,
my father said; he said these things a hundred
times: *My children must become doctors,*
a good profession for the immigrant.
Never fear the sight of blood for God is great.
Those first years in Maryland we quoted him
nightly, as if hope would make us doctors
or repeating English words would replace
a former accent with none. But there was
always the scent of spices on our breath,
and bronze elephants waiting on the front steps.

57

I'm half Bengali, so I went to Calcutta
to find my half-Bengaliness. I scanned
the street for signs. I looked to the light
of the sky, and I sniffed the sooty air
for familiarity; but it smelt null
as home whenever I'd gone back. I took
the city tour to orient myself.
So many conquerors looted the state.
Was I supposed to think my house was robbed?
I was, and I was to be poor forever.
Then at a stop I fell out into the crowd.
It was like falling in love: I wasn't lost.
I saw a man waiting, a discreet shop
manager. I found a city on his face.

[31]

He let a woman on the tram (made room on a stair).
His hand brushed her hip at the banister.
He wanted only to whisper between stops.
Meet me here tomorrow if you can,
I'll wait. While, on the roof,
the conductor's cousins numbered into infinity—
chewing betel, out of work, leaning the other
way as the tram rounded a sharp corner.
Inside, shoulders rubbed against chiffon saris
careening past a million balconies on the roads.
Monuments, relatives, what scale for a city!
Never mind. The manager only thought of this:
she wore a purple sari, her hair was loose,
on her brown arm no bangle keeping her with one man.

Home was where they added strips of tarmac
to the once narrow road. Thirteen, we roved
the streets, Maryellen and I, met up after
school and on Saturdays, her pockets tight
with change and a flirty note, from Donny
or Mike. But at thirteen, they were young for us,
though we'd hope to wave at them on our way.
In love, we courted risk at Seven-Eleven
on Randolph, bikers in their leather pants;
dreamt we'd cycle out at night, while Rock-
ville Pike stuck its neon metals over
cinemas and hot dog stands, and White Oak
brightened with signs under electric stars—
and all night we'd smoke in unlocked cars.

[33]   Into the Capitol
in memory of Maryellen Wendel
(1962–1983)

She'd plan to cross the creek and meet me
at Hollywood where the road turned gravel.
Up the hilly street to Our Place, we'd make
a left, pedal through Venice, and Valley
Brook where the high school was; then pass
St. John's cement Mary and the interminable
brick junior high; we'd race by the dead birds
on the underpass and by the Colesville Sears
where we'd tried lipstick on and jeans. Far down
New Hampshire Avenue into D.C., we'd go
dancing someday or to a show; there was
no doubt about when—it was always next
week-end we'd steal out with money and no
keys, and we promised not to miss anyone.

You might as well have been Tevye, and home
could have been Anatevka. It wasn't a film.
The neighbors miss you, especially the Greeks:
their accent to yours is as baklava to halwah;
as Alexander's green eyes touring India,
and weddings milling in the square, are to laying
almonds, filo, patience, honey. We were more
like our neighbors than we were like anyone else;
but they lived in different terms. They lived in Greek:
inside their house it was Athens again; whereas
we packed suddenly to come, brought only coats
in case the weather turned, and we travelled
till no one heard not even the fiddler playing tunes
at night in Anatevka regardless of the change.

[35]   The Service
                                    for Deepika

We gathered at the university.
Deans, other doctors, friends. She was all
eyes, my sister, spotting a bum in the pew
coolly seated right in front near an aisle.
No usher removed him. No one asked who
he was. His torn shirt and hair all raggedy
were new to us. He didn't know this was
a service and reception for a Hindu
man in America; you couldn't tell
by the sequence of tributes anyway.
No son circling a pyre; no guru to say
who died. We thought the bum was the true
prophet, so lean like one, and he would pray
for us. Later we watched him pocketing food.

If you're hungry, why don't you eat?
If you're tired, why do you work all night?
If you're home, why don't you pick up the phone?
Why do you let it ring eight times?—
One-sided conversations, like wishful
thinking. But you had another language too,
one-man Hindi choir cross-legged
on the temple floor. The shrine was full
of light; and your lips quivered, moving
the flame to the rhythm of your expiration.
The family slept through your early morning
amplification of *oam*, whose range
depended on repetition. . . . Now it's strange
not to miss the man, but his echo.

If *oam* has forms, they will come to us
in the swift insistence of a hologram,
from the eighteenth book of an epic.
Oam is the gruff undertow of a voice,
the ball-bearing deeps of a drawer, a picnic
and flower-strewn handshakes of neighbors in church
(and in fall the low notes of farewell);
oam, the gesture of tide shifting a beach;
and isn't it the breath priests leave to echo
in small places before turning out the ceiling light?—
its string swinging a prayer wheel,
or the earth latched as a pendulum
skimming the atmosphere's hollow aisle
like desire traversing a throat.

When noon struck Maryland, Bombay ticked
at midnight—too late to phone your brother,
so you sent aerograms with Sindhi script
right to left and English phrases left
to right. His eyes would literally flutter
to read your news; and he was known to add
that at least your being gone brought letters.
When you were home, you were always out.

Seems like Sunday you planned to call Anandas.
It is twenty years. Always here and there,
you longed to stay at Bethany in Delaware,
the nearest watery link to the places in your
mind: the flights of steps down to Ganga at
Benares, Hardwar, Gaumuk, Allahabad.

[39]   Chasing Lime
Listen, meditate, appropriate each day.
Why then do you still doubt?
—on a temple wall

I wish I were a better Hindu,
had a Sanskrit name meaning
take your time. In Hindi *kal* means
yesterday and tomorrow. So why hurry?
Only one word for days.
In White Oak I dreamt we bowed
to a pit and pressed a finger on ash
to remind us what a body was.
We tossed flowers to the gods
and the gods tossed back.
Always orange marigolds. At home,
my knees up like rocks in a rumrunner,
your two highballs chasing lime,
you kept repeating, *Sarla, take your time.*

When you were out of town, and the red flag
was turned down, your postcards lay inside
the covered wagon-shaped mailbox. It made
me think of settlers moving west beyond
the reach of mail or a map's torn border.
Your telegrams were short, and with stops
inserted, odd to read, though a card may
not have been much longer than a phrase:
Sarla, missed flight for my minute's delay.
Home soon. You wrote me, *on runways*
swamijis were hawking roses. More
could not be contained on a postcard,
though the flip side showed fantastic
boulevards or a sky's unreal blue.

[41]   Heart Donor

You gave your son his first Erector Set.
Ever since, the house always lacked a hinge—
his loosened closet door on which you leaned
your narcotic frame. Neighbors crowded like crows
on the drive after the medics slipped in—
no siren: or, downstairs we couldn't hear.
But your son would see you smoothly led
down hospital corridors on a chrome-wheeled cot
driving a spirit with no heart: your heart
for science, that we not wonder why a piece
survives a whole; so that someone should use it
as a man would take a tool for the day's work,
as your son used his to unmake latches
and all the other world came into view.

Train Windows
for Derek Walcott

Give me the summary, you said. What did
the journey come to? It came to this:
inheriting your richest lands, words:
moving through the framed spaces, square
train windows out of which I'd always look
for you in your khaki shirt. I'd pretend
the train was near a coast and listen for
your call, but hear myself, as if you were always
near like a rhyme or like one's native tongue;
later, like the sound of type, the click
of words—you let me hear them those days
in Boston. I felt at home again, or
calm among words, their clear panes through which views
peered back as greetings to a traveller.

Glossary

Foreign words are Hindi, unless noted otherwise.

acchar: pickles
agarbati: incense
Amma: mother
anna: before the new rupee (1956), an anna was one-sixteenth of the rupee
baingan: eggplant
barthans: vessels
bhel: a snack
bidi: cigarette
Brahma, Vishnu, Mahesh: one naming of the Hindu trinity
brinjohl (Sindhi): eggplant
chat: a snack
chota-bhai: little brother
chuuni: long scarf, head-covering for women
Divali: Festival of Lights, Hindu
dupatta: see *chuuni*
Durga Puja: Hindu festival celebrating Durga, goddess who destroys evil
fulkas (Sindhi): a bread, like tortillas
Ganesh: the elephant god
Ganga: Ganges
ghagra: floor-length skirt
goonda: villain
Holi: Festival of Color, Hindu
Jalaluddin Rumi: Sufi poet from Konya in Anatolia (Turkey)
kemize: tunic
kofta: spiced meatballs
kulfi: ice cream
Mahesh: another name for Shiva
maidan: field
mali: gardener
Mashi (Bengali): aunt
Nana: maternal grandfather

Nani: maternal grandmother

Oam Sri Ram: invocation to the Lord Rama

paan-wala: tobacco-seller

Parvathi: the goddess who, because she had a negligent husband
   (Lord Shiva), wished a son out of mud. He was given the head
   of an elephant and named Ganesh. From her bath water,
   Parvathi conceived a daughter.

phul: flowers

phul-gobi: flower-cabbage, or cauliflower

pista-badam: pistachio-almond

Puja: Hindu worship service

puri: fried flatbread

rangoli: painted floor decoration

subzi: vegetable

Ulasnagar, Kalyan: Bombay outskirts; postpartition refugee camps
   established especially for Sindhis who left what is now
   Pakistan

wala: a merchant, a type of worker, a fellow

White Elephants has been composed by Wilsted & Taylor in Monotype Bell types and was printed and bound by Malloy Lithographing, Ann Arbor, Michigan.
Book design by Christopher Kuntze.

Printed in the United States
by Baker & Taylor Publisher Services